jam!

The story of jazz music

52nd Street, New York City, was once widely known as the "The Street." At one time, it was the center of the jazz scene.

jam!

The story of jazz music

jeanne lee

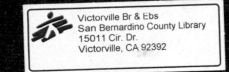

rosen publishing group, inc./new york

Published in 1999 by The Rosen Publishing Group, Inc.
29 East 21st Street, New York, NY 10010

Copyright © 1999 by The Rosen Publishing Group, Inc.

First Edition

Library of Congress Cataloging-in-Publication Data

Lee, Jeanne.
    Jam! : the story of jazz music / Jeanne Lee. — 1st ed.
        p. cm. —(The library of African American arts and culture)
    Includes bibliographical references (p.   ) and index.
    Summary : Describes the history and development of jazz music in America from its roots in Africa to the contemporary music scene.
        ISBN 0-8239-1852-1
        1. Jazz—History and criticism Juvenile literature.   [1. Jazz.]   I. Title.
II. Series.
ML3508.L44 1999
781.65—dc21   99-10973
                                                                      CIP

Manufactured in the United States of America

Contents

Introduction

1942: It's midnight, you're at Minton's Playhouse in Harlem, and the music is hot. Kenny Clarke on drums, Charlie "Bird" Parker on sax, Thelonious Monk on piano, Curley Russell on bass, Dizzy Gillespie on trumpet—they're jamming a song that twists and turns.

Bird peppers the air with short, staccato notes on sax—sometimes right on the beat, sometimes slightly, thrillingly off.

Diz steps forward, raises his trumpet to his lips, and blows: a chill goes down your spine.

These musicians are experimenting in a musical style that would later come to be known as bebop, or bop. Bursting onto the scene in the 1940s, bebop changed the face of music in America. But bebop is only one of many frontiers in the long and rich history of jazz.

Jazz music comes out of the experiences of African Americans. Its roots are in the traditions and rhythms of Africa. When Africans were forced to come to America as slaves, they brought their musical traditions with them. And even during the

A musician performing swing music at a club on 52nd Street in 1939

The musical styles and traditions of Africa have made jazz music what it is today.

ordeal of slavery, African Americans preserved their spirit and culture by keeping music alive.

Over the generations, elements of African music changed by coming into contact with American traditions. This meeting created the right setting for the birth of jazz.

When it was created, jazz was a brand-new kind of music. Because it allows freedom for improvisation, or inventing things as you go along, it has blossomed into many different styles. Swing, big band, bebop, free jazz, and fusion are just a few of the many styles of jazz.

In this book you will travel back in time to Africa and discover the roots of jazz. You will then journey forward and see how traditional African music grew in America. You'll learn more about what jazz is, where it came from, and how it took the world by storm.

7

1 the african tradition

Jazz music was born in America. But the ancestors of the first jazz players came from Africa, a land of rich culture and great beauty.

A Majestic Land

The physical terrain of Africa is vast and exquisite. The central African region, the Congo Basin, contains most of the African rain forests. There are additional rain forests growing along the coastal areas of West Africa as far as the Guinea coast; and to the east as far as the highlands of Ethiopia, Kenya, Burundi, Rwanda, and Tanzania; and on the island of Madagascar off the coast of Tanzania. Africa also has many savanna grasslands. The deserts of Africa are the Sahara in the north and the Kalahari in the south.

Music and dance are a central part of the many cultures of Africa.

Ocean

Civilization and Culture

Although Africa is home to many different peoples, they share various aspects of a common culture. Traditionally, for most people agriculture (farming) was the basis of the economy. People also had an area of specialization—iron and woodworking; basket and cloth weaving; barbering; leather work; soap, oil, and pottery making; or fishing— based on the natural resources of their region.

The economic system was based on bartering (trading goods for other goods) along with the use of the cowrie shell as money. Social and economic organization covered the spectrum from extended family units to independent village-states to territorial empires like ancient Sudan, Ghana, Mali, Songhay, and Ethiopia. Most of these units had their own armies and courts. Land belonged to the community, and its resources and responsibilities were shared.

cowrie shells

Even although most African languages were spoken and not written, the Egyptians, the Ethiopians, the Vai of Liberia, and the Ejagham of southwestern Cameroon and southwestern Nigeria all had written languages. The University of Timbuktu was famous throughout the ancient world as a center of learning. It was mentioned in European and North African histories as a place where historical, medical, legal, and religious manuscripts in Greek, Latin, Arabic, and Sudanese were kept.

The traditional religious beliefs of many African cultures began with a Supreme God who created the earth. Then came a category of other gods who represented natural forces, including human life forces, and then a strata of ancestors. All life was thought to possess, in fragmented and individualized form, a piece of the life force of the Supreme God, which continued even after a person's death.

Music

Like religion, the arts were another form of life expression. Song, music, and dance have always been closely connected in African culture. Songs were sung while people worked at different tasks—hunting, fishing, farming, foraging, ironwork, and woodwork. Songs were also an important part of festivals, prayer, and funerals. Warriors would perform war dances and

Egyptian hieroglyphics: an ancient written language of North Africa

FACE A.

sing of bravery and daring. Griots were traveling singers who recited history from memory and passed it down from generation to generation. A griot was a kind of traveling newscaster as well, commenting on the events of the day. In fact, sometimes a griot was paid to stop singing due to the embarrassment of the person who was the target of the song.

The Voice

The main instrument people used to make music was the human voice. Many African languages are tonal languages. That means that you can change the meaning of a word by saying (or singing) the syllables in a high, medium, or low tone. For example, "ol or un lo da m" could either mean "God made me" or "God betrayed me" depending on the length and tone of the syllables.

The African singing voice can

Although there are many different styles in African music, there is one basic belief: that the nature of existence is energy, or different life forces that are always in motion.

The highest achievement of art (music, sculpture, dance, weaving, metal or woodworking, painting) is to portray this underlying motion or life-force.

range from growls, whispers, grunts, or shouts to a falsetto (a high, "false" voice). The emphasis is on a person's individual expression rather than on a standard pitch or sound.

Two of the song types sung in Africa had a special influence later on in America. One of these song types was the field holler, sometimes spelled hollar. People often sang a holler in order to communicate while they were working outdoors. It was not so much a song as a wordless cry that could be carried across the fields on the wind. It could be a cry of grief, loneliness, or happiness, or it might be a request for help. At other times it may have been used as a warning signal. Often another person would respond with his or her own holler.

Call-and-response was another type of song. A lead singer would set the pace with the "call" part of the song. The "response," a repeated refrain or phrase, was then given by a group. This style of music resembles the rhythm of conversation: One person speaks; the other answers.

Sometimes a response would include extra commentary on a person or event. This variation could cause the call and the response to overlap.

The Drum

Another instrument used in Africa was the

This drum from Ghana was carved from a tree trunk base and has leather stretched over the top.

drum. The drum provided beats for people to sing and dance to. When beats or sounds occur in a pattern, they create a rhythm. These beats can be stressed or unstressed, long or short.

In traditional African music, beats were carried by a chorus of drummers. A master drummer would improvise new rhythms to add to the basic drum choir rhythms.

Sounds that closely resemble the tones of speech can be made on the drum. A good drummer can actually communicate through his instrument by using rhythms. He can make his drum sing the different tones of his language and then combine them with the natural rhythms of a sentence. This allows the drum to "talk."

The drum was not the only instrument used in traditional African music, however. Other percussion instruments like the balaphon (a keyboard of wood

A chorus of African drummers

strung together with calabash or gourd resonators underneath to amplify the sound) were the precursors to the marimba, xylophone, and vibra-

phone. The kalimba (or "thumb piano"), with iron tongues attached to a wooden resonator box, is another example of tuned keyboards belonging to the percussion family. The kalimba makes a sound when it is struck, either by a stick or with the hands.

A balaphon is played with mallets like a xylophone.

An Oral Tradition

Music in Africa is an oral tradition. That means that it is passed by word of mouth from mother to child, grandfather to grandchild, teacher to student. Due to this oral tradition, a good memory has always been a prized and necessary asset in African culture.

This oral tradition played a very important part in the history of African Americans. As you will see in the following chapters, when Africans were brutally captured by Europeans and brought to the Americas as slaves starting in the 1600s, they were able to preserve their music and their heritage by using their memory. Against all odds, music was carried in their hearts and minds.

The Talking Drum

The most well known of the drum "families" is the "talking drum," an hourglass-shaped wooden base with animal skin drum-heads at both ends. These drum-heads are held on by cords, usually of animal hide, that connect them to each other along the length of the drum. When held between the drummer's side and forearm and squeezed or released, it produces higher and lower tones. When the drum-head is struck with a wooden hooked stick, it produces speech-like tones.

These drums vary in size. The smaller drums having a higher range of pitches, often used in ceremonies for women and girls. The larger and deeper toned drums were used in ceremonies for men and boys.

Other tonal drums are the log or slit drums. Drums similar to the conga and bongos of Latin America were played in pairs. Accompanying these drums were various shaken instruments like rattles, usually made from gourds, seeds, shells, and metal bells.

2 africans in america

Beginning in the 1600s and over the 200 years that followed, approximately 10 to 15 million Africans were brutally taken from their homeland and brought to the Americas. About 500,000 of these Africans were taken on a grueling ship journey to what is now the United States. The route these slave ships followed is known as the Middle Passage.

The slave trade had a devastating effect on African culture. Traditions were disrupted, villages were broken apart, and customs and religions were disregarded. People of the same culture and even family members were separated. African Americans were made slaves for life. They were viewed as property, not as human beings.

Slavery in America had a deep and sorrowful impact on the lives of Africans and their African American descendants. During the time of slavery,

Captive Africans arriving in America to be sold as slaves

important aspects of African life and tradition were forbidden. Many slave owners outlawed the drum because it could be used as a means of communication. African ritual and ceremony were also widely forbidden.

However, African culture did not simply die out. Instead African traditions were adapted to these new circumstances. The music of Africa began to change; new songs and instruments developed.

The Work Song

Like their forefathers and foremothers in Africa, African Americans sang while working in order to make the time pass more quickly. This type of song came to be known as the work song.

The work song often carried the African influence of the call-and-response and field holler styles. The rhythm of the task brought out the feeling of the music. Workers punctuated the laying of the railroad ties by coordinating a hammer swing with a chorus based on the grunt of effort. While rowing boats, people echoed the drag of the oar in the water by stretching the syllable they were singing, then catching up with the rhythm and keeping the beat intact.

Slave owners and their appointed overseers were quick to take advantage of the group effort led by singing. When slaves sang a slow song, they would be ordered to sing faster. Slaves who had ability as a lead

Berta, when you marry,
don't marry that,
railroad man, lordy
whoa-ah

every day a Sunday dollar,
in your hand, lordy
well now -

"HOOKING-UP."

A group of slaves at work on a sugar plantation

singer could increase the group's productivity. Therefore they would be bought and sold for a higher price.

Since it was considered rebellious to speak outrightly of freedom, slaves used words in songs to tell of their thoughts and mistreatment. The lyrics of the work song were often a disguised way for workers to criticize the conditions and people around them. The commentary on the overseer, the owner, and their families and friends was done indirectly, often through animal tales. This indirectness saved the slaves from punishment.

When African Americans sang work songs it seemed to European American observers that certain notes seemed to "bend" or "slur." To some of these people it sounded as if the voices were "off pitch." But really, these notes were sung according to an African kind of musical scale that many Europeans had never heard before.

These different, "flattened" notes are the parents of what is called the "blue note." A blue note has an incredibly moving effect on a listener. Instrumentalists and vocalists embrace the blue note and "blue scales" to create a compelling emotional feel in jazz music.

New Instruments

Although the drum was outlawed by many slave owners, African Americans adopted new instruments. These new forms of music also echoed the song traditions of Africa. Certain techniques—such as sliding the fingers on the frets of a guitar or banjo—create a sound much like the wail of a field cry. Instruments used in jazz, like the keyboards and wind instruments, were made to sound like the human voice as well.

During the era of slavery, new musical forms began to develop that paved the way for jazz.

3 parents of jazz

Spirituals

Many early styles of African American music inspired jazz. One important early musical form was the spiritual, a kind of religious folk song.

Spirituals were born as slaves began to adopt Christianity. Slaves learned popular hymns (religious poems based on the Psalms and set to music) and added their own singing styles and their own words.

Spirituals often included call-and-response-type singing. Slow spirituals, called "sorrow songs," were sung in a heavy style very close to speech. But other spirituals, called jubilees, took on a more lively rhythm. They later became an important ingredient in jazz.

In that great getting up morning
fare you well
fare you well!

t great getting up morning
fare you well
fare you well!

Fisk Jubilee Singers

The Fisk Jubilee Singers, of Fisk University in Nashville, Tennessee, were a group of African American students who toured the United States and Europe in 1871 to raise money for their university. Of the nine original members, seven had been slaves. They sang slave spirituals such as "Go Down, Moses" as well as songs more familiar to white audiences, such as "Old Folks at Home." As a result, they were helping to bring two musical worlds together.

The Fisk Jubilee Singers were a smash success, giving deeply moving performances that won rave reviews from critics and attracted wide audiences. Through their tours, the Fisk Jubilee Singers succeeded in raising $150,000 for the Fisk University building program. They also introduced the music of African Americans to people who had never heard it before.

Minstrels and Songsters

Minstrels and songsters also inspired the development of jazz.

In the late 1800s, some African Americans began to make a living as traveling performers.

Minstrels appeared in early colonial times, when people performed in variety shows (called tent shows because they were staged under large tents). Minstrels entertained audiences by telling musical stories and ballads and performing songs, dances, and skits.

Many early minstrels were actually white performers who would put on "blackface." These performers made themselves up to look like unrealistic caricatures of African Americans by smearing burnt cork on their faces. But soon African Americans began to use minstrel shows as a way to earn a living as professional entertainers. By the end of the 1800s, African Americans had formed their own minstrel companies.

Wandering singer-performers, or songsters, were

23

also popular in the 1800s. You can compare them to the griots, the wandering songsters of Africa. Any place could serve as a stage for a traveling songster: a street corner, a tavern, or a community gathering. A songster's ballad might have been a romantic or adventuresome song about legendary black heroes such as John Henry or infamous outlaws such as Stagolee.

Songsters often had instrumentalists to accompany them. But over time the songsters preferred to accompany themselves. This later, guitar-toting generation of songsters formed a bridge between earlier black music and the blues

Blues

The blues was born in the early 1900s. Blues was usually about bad times, fears, woes, hard luck, and love (often lost). Blues singers were some of the first people in America to sing about taboo subjects such as drinking, gam-

W. C. Handy made history when he published the first blues sheet music, "Memphis Blues," in 1912. One of his later popular blues songs, "St. Louis Blues," helped this musical style gain a wide audience.

bling, jail, and prostitution. As with work songs, blues verses were improvised—made up as singers went along, depending on how they were feeling.

Blues singers sang of hard times. However, they often exaggerated their woes or gave them a dash of humor. Some blues musicians say that you cannot play the blues properly unless you are feeling blue and that only by singing the blues can you get rid of them!

Blues music laid the groundwork for jazz in its use of riffs and breaks. Riffs are single rhythmic phrases repeated over and over—sometimes as a background to the melody and other times as the actual melody. Breaks are places in the music in which a musician "breaks" away and plays a solo, making it up as he goes along.

Ragtime

Ragtime, another parent of jazz, also came about in the beginning of the twentieth century. Most American

Bessie Smith sang a sassy style of blues called urban blues, which was the first to be widely recorded. Meanwhile, songsters and their descendants popularized another style of blues, rural blues, which had its roots in sorrow songs.

households had a piano during this time, just as most homes have televisions today. Although many African Americans couldn't afford to take piano lessons, they learned to play by ear. The result—ragtime—was piano music with a special kind of jumping rhythm. This rhythm was unique because it was syncopated. This means it had a **shift** of accent from the **strong beat** to the weak beat that lasted throughout the whole song.

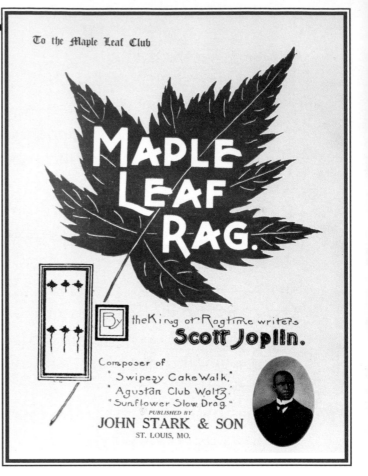

An African American composer, Scott Joplin, made ragtime popular when he wrote and published the "Maple Leaf Rag" in 1899. Many ragtime tunes, such as "The Entertainer," are still played by high school marching bands.

Ragtime became popular by way of great musicians such as Jelly Roll Morton—later considered a pioneer of jazz. He had a strong influence on other jazz pianists such as Fats Waller, Willie "the Lion" Smith, and James P. Johnson.

4 the new orleans scene

New Orleans, Louisiana, is considered the cradle of jazz. The music of New Orleans developed at the very same time as the various styles you read about in the last chapter. It later became the spark that ignited jazz.

New Orleans was a unique American city because it was home to people of many different cultures: European Americans, especially French and Spanish, who had settled in Louisiana generations earlier; Creoles of color (people who are a mixture of French and/or Spanish, as well as African, heritage); and African American slaves.

Many of the wealthier people of New Orleans had knowledge of, and training in, classical music. At the same time, poorer people played French and Spanish-influenced songs by ear for fun. These musical forms, in turn, also mixed in elements from the amazing music-making of Congo Square.

Canal Street, New Orleans, Louisiana, 1890s

Congo Square

Congo Square in New Orleans was a place in which plantation slaves were able to gather on Sundays to sing and dance. The dancing would start with a slow shuffle step in a circle around the musicians. As the day wore on, the chanting and dancing

dancing the bamboula

would build in excitement—until, after reaching a total frenzy, people would faint from exhaustion.

Instruments used in a Congo Square celebration included different kinds of drums; a long-necked lute (whose origins may have been the Congo); an instrument descended from the kalimba or thumb piano; a four-stringed banjo as well as assorted gourds, rattles, and scrapers from West and central Africa.

Even after slavery was abolished, Congo Square had a lasting impact on the city's music.

A percussion instrument made from a dried gourd, covered with a net of woven seeds

Coming Together

The rhythms of Congo Square were being picked up by the orchestras and bands of New Orleans. This was true especially of the popular marching bands that traveled through the city with people following and dancing behind them. Trumpeter Bunk Johnson reported that by 1889, the musicians from downtown New Orleans were playing regularly with the uptown musicians in funerals, parades, and dances.

As a result, dances such as the French square dance, known as the quadrille, were coming together with Afro-Spanish rhythms like the tango and rhumba. Musicians who were trained in European classical music, and those whose music had a more traditional African feel, were also meeting up.

African Americans incorporated Western and African instruments and dances into new musical styles.

The Drums of Congo Square

The rhythms that the drummers beat out in the dusty sunlight made the people standing around want to move their heads in time, tap their feet, and dance, too. That is one of the things about jazz: it always makes people want to move. Jazz music is music to move to, to dance to—not just to listen to.

—Langston Hughes

IN THE STORE.

29

By the early 1900s, classically trained Creoles of color, such as clarinetists Lorenz Tio, Alphonse Picou, and trombonist Kid Ory joined forces with the "rougher" playing uptown musicians like clarinetist Sidney Bechet and trumpeter Buddy Bolden. They learned from each other by listening. The result was a kind of music that had never been heard before. First known as "jass," it later came to be known as jazz.

Sidney Bechet

jazz
catching
fire

Although many ingredients
came together to make jazz,
jazz sounds like nothing else.
That's because jazz is a way of playing, a way of *feeling* music. A song
can be played or sung in a happy,
teasing, way, in a soulful, "blue"
way, or any way in-between.

Chicago and
New York

Jazz was beginning
to spread from New Orleans to other parts of the
country. Many musicians moved to Chicago during
World War I (1917-1921), making it another capital
of jazz. This new music was starting to be recorded,
too, which helped it to catch on.

Dancers enjoying jazz music at the Savoy Ballroom in
Harlem, New York City.

Meanwhile, New York—always a haven for black musicians—started to become a haven for jazz. The Harlem Renaissance of the 1920s, an African American intellectual movement, encouraged the work of artists in many fields. As a result, it helped to foster this new musical form.

What Makes Jazz?

Improvisation. Instead of being played strictly from written notes, much of jazz is improvised, or made up as the musicians go along.

Syncopation. In syncopated music, rhythms are created in which the emphasis shifts from the strong beat to the weak beat, or so that the different rhythms play with each other.

Blue note. A bent or slurred note. Playing blue notes will create unique harmonies and often will convey a deeply emotional feel.

Complex Rhythm. Rhythm is made not only by a drum, but by the accents played by different members of a jazz ensemble.

Two Pioneers

Many unknown musicians contributed to the development
of jazz. But the following
two people are con-
sidered among the
foremost legends
of jazz music.

Louis Armstrong

Louis
Armstrong's life
spanned almost
the entire history
of jazz in this
century. Growing
up in New Orleans,
he wanted to play
the horn but couldn't
afford one. Only when he
was sent to reform school
was he able to play in the school's
Coloured Waifs' Band. He had to wait almost a year
for that privilege!

After he left reform school, Armstrong didn't pick up

Louis Armstrong

a horn again until he was about sixteen. But the rest is history. He soon made a name for himself in New Orleans, both for his superb cornet playing and for his funny, gravelly singing voice. Louis's big break came when, in 1922, the renowned bandleader King Oliver sent for Armstrong to join him in Chicago with his King Oliver's Creole Jazz Band.

Louis Armstrong became a top-notch jazz soloist. He influenced not only other horn players, but also other instrumentalists and vocalists around the world. Armstrong had an ability to make his cornet "sing"—to tell a story with warmth and human feeling.

Armstrong's work with blues singers can be heard on recordings with Ma Rainey and Bessie Smith. The recordings of Smith and Armstrong later inspired the singing of the great jazz vocalist Billie Holiday. Armstrong also led groups of his own: The Hot Fives, The Hot Sevens, and The Armstrong Stompers, which featured Earl "Fatha" Hines on piano.

Later in life Armstrong became an

Louis Armstrong playing at the pyramids in Eygpt

34

emblem of American jazz. He was sponsored by the State Department on several tours around the world. He is said to have especially treasured his 1960 tour of Africa, where crowds carried him on their shoulders.

Duke Ellington

Edward Kennedy "Duke" Ellington was another individual to occupy a unique place in jazz.

Edward Kennedy Ellington had been a painting student before he developed an interest in music, sparked by hearing James P. Johnson's "Carolina Shout" as a teenager. From that point on, he began to take his piano lessons more seriously. As a

Duke Ellington and his Cotton Club orchestra in New York City

mature musician he used his band to paint pictures in sound, describing the entire spectrum of the African American experience.

Instead of being a soloist, Ellington was a bandleader. He used variety in his arrangements and included call-and-response as an important part of his band's sound. He credits the New Orleans influence with shaping his vision. Several of his soloists—Sidney Bechet, clarinetist Barney Bigard, and trumpeter Bubber Miley—were New Orleans musicians. Ellington used innovative ways of blending the instruments to get a special "color," or emotional sound.

From 1927 to 1932, Ellington led the house band at The Cotton Club in Harlem, New York City, playing for dance productions and revues. These shows were broadcast nightly, contributing to his popularity.

Ellington is credited with inventing the jazz ballad. Before him, the only slow compositions were blues and spirituals. Ellington was also famous for integrating the musical personalities of his players into his arrangements and compositions.

Big Band and the Swing Era

As you can tell from the life of Duke Ellington, the face of jazz had begun to change. One new aspect was that, during the 1920s, larger orchestras called "big bands" began to assemble.

Unlike the early jazz players, many of the big band musicians had received formal musical training. And unlike the small, New Orleans-style bands that improvised, big bands relied on written music with only occasional room for solo improvisation. This was partly because jazz music was being recorded and broadcast over the radio. It had to hold to a strict time schedule in order to fit on a record or radio program.

Two of the musicians widely acknowledged for initiating the big band era are pianist Fletcher Henderson and saxophonist Don Redman. Together they collaborated on musical arrangements for Henderson's big band, which became the dance band at New York's Roseland Ballroom. Other big bands began to spring up across the United States.

Kansas City came to be known as a jazz hub. Kansas City had a unique sound because it was a meeting ground for musicians of many different geographic and musical backgrounds: New Orleans jazzmen, blues musicians from the Mississippi Delta, and traveling East Coast players. The resulting sound was heavily influenced by the blues, because that was a good common ground for these diverse musicians. They would start a piece by playing together, and then they would take turns improvising the chorus. At the end of a piece they would join together again.

One of the greatest big

it don't mean a thing
if you ain't
got that swing

William "Count" Basie seated at the piano with another legendary bandleader, Benny Goodman, and singer Ethel Waters band leaders, Count Basie, had the Kansas City sound. Count Basie brought this blues sensibility into his big band format, using call-and-response in riffs between sections and creating a smooth and driving rhythm section.

A style of jazz called swing emerged. Swing was characterized by a steady and lively rhythm. Popularized by the Benny Goodman Orchestra, the Duke Ellington Orchestra, the Count Basie Orchestra, and the Tommy Dorsey Orchestra, swing ushered in what has come to be known as the golden age of jazz.

During the golden age of jazz, a wagon loaded with jazz musicians rolls through Times Square in New York City.

ART TATUM

Onward

By the 1940s, New York City had become the center of the jazz world. Jazz clubs such as the Onyx, the Downbeat, and Birdland lined 52nd Street, hosting all of the hottest players. At the same time, clubs such as the Apollo Theater and the Savoy Ballroom uptown in Harlem were alive with music and dancing.

It was only a matter of time before jazz would take a new turn.

Pianist Art Tatum essentially recomposed songs, changing melodies, harmonies, chord voicings, and rhythms from chorus to chorus. He seemed to have the ability to turn the piano into an orchestra.

6 bebop and beyond

During the 1940's, when New York became a jazz center, many changes were taking place in society. For one, the United States was fighting World War II. Money was very tight, and big bands had become too expensive to maintain. At the same time, the vinyl used for making records was needed by the defense industry, and record production ground to a halt.

While this "commercial" side of jazz was temporarily on hold, musicians continued to experiment with different kinds of playing.

Small ensembles began to replace the expensive big bands. In New York, at clubs such as Minton's Playhouse, a new kind of jazz began to take shape. Charlie Parker, the great saxophone player known as "Bird," was one of the inventors of this brand of jazz, called bebop. Bebop got its name from its unusual sounds and rhythms.

In swing music, the kind of jazz that was popular before bebop, the rhythms were fluid and seemed to move easily from one phrase to another. The musicians who invented bebop did not want their music to sound that agreeable. They added accents in the rhythm that made the beat jagged and surprising. Saying

Dizzy Gillespie

Charlie Parker

the word "bebop" out loud can give you some idea of the feel of that style of music.

Legends

Musicians who started in the bop era became legends in their own time. Many of them continued to develop their music through many years and styles.

The saxophonist Charles "Bird" Parker was a major influence in jazz. Parker methodically taught himself to play the scales in every key, a half step at a time, and the blues in all keys.

Bird's phrasing, innovation, and breakneck speed are legendary. The blues remained a cornerstone of his playing. He invented new melodies for others' compositions as well as his own tunes, often giving the resulting piece a new name.

Toward the end of his life, Parker began to include certain musical elements in his compositions—such as bitonality (playing in two keys at the same time), extended harmonies, and innovative note sequences—

43

that would inspire the next generation of reed players, including Ornette Coleman, John Coltrane, and Eric Dolphy.

Thelonious Monk

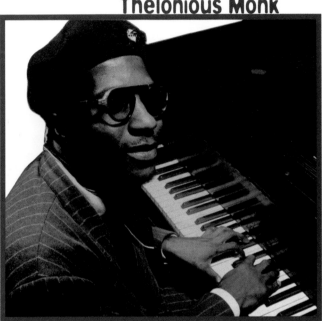

Parker's choice of notes and phrasing often imitated speech. This often lent itself to verbal interpretation. Singers such as Eddie Jefferson, King Pleasure, and Dave Lambert, Jon Hendricks, and Annie Ross (of Lambert, Hendricks, and Ross) put words to several of Parker's solos.

Another creator of bop, pianist Thelonious Monk, composed and improvised music using his keen intuition. His music was marked by subtle dynamics and sharp, angular melodies that started, stopped, and developed in unexpected ways.

Kenny Clarke made innovations on how the drums interacted within a jazz group. When instrumentalists played asymmetrical (uneven) phrases, improvised on riffs, played across bar lines, and used alternate melodies and chords, Clarke (or "Klook-mop," later shortened to "Klook") began to make the sound of the drum more transparent. By playing the rhythm on cymbals—especially the ride cymbal—he kept the sound light. He used the tom, snare, and bass drums for accents and punctuation. This allowed the other instruments to be heard more clearly.

Trumpeter Dizzy Gillespie became a leader in the bop movement, in particular as the bandleader of the quintet at the Onyx Club, from which bebop got its name. He continued to explore new musical territories, such as Afro-Cuban rhythms, and became yet another icon of jazz.

The Jazz Vocalists

The popular jazz vocalists of the thirties, forties, and fifties were crucial in popularizing jazz.

Ella Fitzgerald got her start with Chick Webb's band at the Savoy Ballroom. Her Songbook series— with composers George and Ira Gershwin, Cole Porter, Duke Ellington, and others—and her famous recordings with Louis Armstrong on Verve records showcased her top-notch rhythm. Her joyous voice and swinging approach to

Dizzy Gillespie on "The Street"

Billie Holiday

popular songs earned her the title of First Lady of Song.

The singer Sarah Vaughan, also known as "Sassy," had originally been the pianist with the Billy Eckstine band. Vaughan was able to transcend the category of jazz singer. With her rich, unlimited tone and range, she also appealed to popular and classical music audiences.

Billie Holiday is credited with making the jazz vocalist's expression sound deeply personal. Almost as famous for her personal struggles as she was for her emotive voice, she also wrote timeless compositions such as "God Bless

Sarah Vaughan

SCAT!

Scatting—the singing of nonsense syllables, or new words instead of the written ones—has become a hallmark of jazz vocals. Sarah Vaughan was famous for her scatting on bop compositions, expertly keeping pace with musicians. Ella Fitzgerald was also famous for her elegant scats. In a recording of Ella's concerts in Berlin, you can listen to her happily scat her way through the song "Mack the Knife" when she forgets the words!

Call-and-Response in jazz

Call-and-response can be heard in jazz when the instruments "trade fours" (or eights or twos). Trading fours means that a musician plays or sings four measures or bars of music, usually following the melody or harmony of a piece of music. Then, another player or singer steps in and and sings or plays the next four measures. Call-and-response also can be heard when one or more members of a jazz ensemble responds to, or "comments" on, the lead voice or soloist's line.

the Child." It was said of one of her performances at Jazz at the Philharmonic that Holiday was able to stretch time until it almost broke.

Nina Simone, a vocalist with a resonant, soul-penetrating voice, became famous for singing songs of all styles, from urban-style blues such as "I Want a Little Sugar in My Bowl," to covers of Bob Dylan and other contemporary songwriters, to her own compositions.

Birth of the Cool
A style of jazz called "cool

The Modern Jazz Quartet was one of many West Coast groups that defined "cool jazz."

Miles Davis

During the fifties, trumpeter Miles Davis began to emerge from his role as Charlie Parker's sideman and to forge an identity that lasted through many years and several styles of jazz. During Davis's lifetime he was able to project his sound and sense of space into bebop, cool jazz, rock-inspired fusion, gospel-influenced jazz called funk or soul jazz, and even electric and rap music.

Despite all the styles of jazz with which he has been associated, Davis always retained the outdoor quality of the field holler and the blues. One of his later recordings, a duet with country blues guitarist-singer John Lee Hooker, captures the essence of this remarkable sound.

jazz" came into popularity in the late 1940s. This lyrical style was sometimes called West Coast jazz due to the high concentration of musicians involved who were employed in the Hollywood studio industry.

Pianists Lennie Tristano, Bill Evans, and Dave Brubeck; saxophonists Paul Desmond, Lee Konitz, and Stan Getz; trumpeter Chet Baker, and the Modern Jazz Quartet were, to various degrees and in differing blends, part of the "cool" style. Miles Davis's recordings in this style, such as "Sketches of Spain," "Porgy and Bess," and "Birth of the Cool," have had a lasting impact on the jazz tradition.

On the opposite end of the spectrum from the "cool" styles were gospel-influenced and soul jazz styles played by musicians like drummer Art Blakey, pianist Horace Silver, and their Jazz Messengers. Tenor saxophonist Sonny Rollins has a penetrating and robust style that began developing in the mid-fifties. He also composed jazz calypsos, drawing from the west Indian background of his mother's family.

Free Jazz

Later in this era, the free jazz style came to prominence. The free jazz sensibility included more of a feel for exotic world music, and it broke away from previous notions about tone and meter. Yet in many ways free jazz was also a return to roots, using elements of the field holler and blues.

Charles Mingus

The bassist Charles Mingus wrote extended musical compositions that used the entire spectrum of African American music, from gospel and blues through bebop, to express political, social, and personal feelings about the world around him. He also brought new elements into music

Charles Mingus

like the sounds of traffic, played by the horns and rhythm section. In a famous duet with multi-reedist Eric Dolphy, Mingus was able to mimic the conversational tones of human speech.

Inspired by African music, Mingus integrated vocal shouts into musical compositions. He and his band members would engage in call-and-response comments, or Mingus would add his voice to a horn section crescendo to heighten the dramatic tension of a piece.

Instead of using sheet music, Mingus used memorization to teach his compositions to members of his groups. He taught the musicians by rote because he wanted them to liberate themselves from the page, internalize the music, and play from the heart.

John Coltrane

During the mid-fifties, tenor saxophonist John Coltrane began to emerge from Miles Davis's quintet to lead groups of his own. By 1960, having absorbed the languages of rhythm 'n' blues, Duke Ellington, bebop, and modal improvisation, Coltrane began using these ingredients to express a growing sense of spirituality.

Coltrane studied Eastern religions and ragas, pieces of Indian classical music. He also began to use elements of the traditional music of Africa, India, and the Near East. He aimed for religious ecstasy through trance and repetition.

One of his most famous compositions, *A Love Supreme*, with its four sections—"Acknowledgement," "Resolution," "Pursuance," and "Psalm"—is an example of Coltrane's use of music as a form of meditation and prayer.

Ornette Coleman

During the sixties many players began to challenge the boundaries of improvisation. Ornette Coleman's listening experiences while growing up included folk music played on kazoo and combs, and Mexican, European, and African American styles of music.

Blues, as well as rhythm 'n' blues, were at the heart of Coleman's playing. He stressed collective improvisation—shared responsibility for the sound and duration of the music being played. In his groups people were encouraged to play from their own imagination.

Other Pioneers

During the 1960s two composer-pianists emerged whose styles were so personal, that they belong in a category all their own.

Sun Ra, born Herman Blount, went from arranging (and filling in at the piano) in the 1940s with the Fletcher Henderson big band in Chicago to leading his own orchestra, which he called his Arkestra. With this Arkestra, Sun Ra found new ways of improvising within the big band format that included costumes and dancers, and he recorded albums such as "The Heliocentric Worlds of Sun Ra" and "Nothing Is."

Cecil Taylor

Cecil Taylor also associates dance with his music. During the 1970s he collaborated with dancer-choreographer Diane MacIntyre's Sounds in Motion company. His music reflects the drumming traditions of African music, from cascades of sound energy to suddenly crystal-clear single notes and silence.

Don Cherry

Other members of the free jazz style of playing—such as tenor saxophonist Archie Shepp, alto saxophonist Albert Ayler, and trumpeter Don Cherry— contributed to post-bop jazz.

Shepp builds upon spirituals, blues, rhythm 'n' blues, gospel exhortation, swing, and bop and uses them as a reference point for open-ended and free improvisation. His tone is large and warm, like that of Coleman Hawkins and Ben Webster, and it is as texturally varied as human speech.

Ayler saw jazz as spiritual music. He is credited with playing free jazz by extending folk music and spirituals beyond their tonal relationships in order to achieve pure emotion in sound.

Cherry also found folk music a source of inspiration and is known for his early work with Ornette Coleman. He has since studied African, Indian, Turkish, and Brazilian music. He composes and plays a synthesis of world music and jazz with musicians from many cultures.

7 looking to the future

New generations of artists have grown out of jazz. In many ways, jazz has both influenced and merged with mainstream popular music, gaining even more widespread appeal. In the 1970s and 1980s the fusion and acid styles of jazz took on many of the sounds of rock 'n' roll. In the recent swing revival, young people started cutting up the dance floor. Hip hop musicians use digital technology to sample jazz and funk music, inserting short clips of old standards into new songs.

New Horizons

Even more traditional artists are expanding the horizons of jazz. Vocalists such as Bobby McFerrin, Cassandra Wilson, and Diana Krall have become well known in our time, and each has taken a different approach. McFerrin, best known for his hit "Don't, Worry Be Happy," has also collaborated with soloists and orchestras that play European classical music. Wilson covers artists from Robert Johnson to Joni Mitchell to the Monkees, sings jazz standards, and writes her own songs. Diana Krall has paid respect to the Nat King Cole trio in the album *All for You*, has followed up with the best-selling *Love Scenes*, and has even appeared on *Melrose Place*. Other young artists such as Holly Cole and Erykah Badu

Toni Morrison receives her 1993 Nobel Prize for Literature from King Carl Gustav December 10, 1993 in Stockholm, Sweden.

are influenced by rhythm 'n blues and pop music.

At the same time, instrumentalists such as Ravi Coltrane, Herbie Hancock, Roy Hargrove, Wynton Marsalis, and Christian McBride continue to introduce new innovations in jazz instrumentals. While finding their own paths, they also nod to those who came before them. Herbie Hancock, for example, has released a CD of jazz ballads by George and Ira Gershwin.

Inspiration

Artists of other disciplines have been drawn to jazz and translate it into their work. For example, Nobel Prize winner Toni Morrison carries jazz elements into written language in her novel *Beloved*. She uses riffs that call and respond, motifs that occur in new ways, and rhythmic dialogue and description.

Jazz is echoed in the syncopated patterns of painting, the jumping feel of graffiti art, and more. Jazz is a musical form so deep and rich, that it continues to renew itself, other music, and the lives of those who hear it. At first a brand-new sound, jazz is now also a tradition.

Glossary

ballad A slow song or musical composition.

bebop A style of jazz marked by rhythmic accents and a jagged beat.

big band A style of jazz played by large orchestras, which relied on written music.

blues A type of music in which rhythmic phrases are repeated; also characterized by songs about hard times and bad luck.

call-and-response An African song type in which a lead singer calls out and the group answers with a repeated phrase.

cool jazz A lyrical type of jazz that became popular in the late 1940s; also called West Coast jazz.

field holler An African song type that people used to communicate with each other while they were working outdoors.

free jazz A style of jazz marked by a sense of mysticism and a return to African roots.

frets ridges on the fingerboard of a stringed instrument (a guitar, for example).

fusion A more recent musical style that blends elements of jazz with rock music.

griots Traveling singers in Africa who would recite history from memory and comment on current events.

improvisation When musicians invent things as they go along.

ragtime A type of piano music marked by a "jumping," syncopated rhythm.

rhythm 'n' blues A kind of modern music influenced by blues and folk music and marked by a strong beat.

riffs Single rhythmic phrases repeated over and over, used in blues and jazz.

scatting Singing nonsense syllables or making up new words instead of singing the written ones.

songsters Wandering singer-performers who would sing ballads about African American heroes and adventures.

soul jazz A gospel-influenced style of jazz; also called funk.

spirituals An African American religious folk song, which later influenced jazz.

swing A style of jazz characterized by a steady, lively, and fluid rhythm.

syncopation When the accent of a rhythm shifts from the strong beat to the weak beat; used in ragtime.

Discography

Armstrong, Louis. *Verve Jazz Masters*. Verve 1994.

Baker, Chet. *My Funny Valentine*. Blue Note 1994.

Basie, Count . *April in Paris*. Verve 1997.

Bechet, Sidney. *Best of*. Blue Note 1994.

Brubeck, Dave. *Time Out*. Columbia/Legacy 1997.

Coleman, Ornette. *The Shape of Jazz to Come*. Rhino 1959.

Coltrane, John. *Giant Steps*. Atlantic 1990.

Coltrane, John. *A Love Supreme*. Impulse 1964.

Coltrane, Ravi. *Moving Pictures*. RCA Victor 1998.

Davis, Miles. *Kind of Blue*. Columbia/Legacy 1997.

Davis, Miles. *Birth of the Cool*. Capitol Jazz 1950.

Ellington, Duke. *The Best of Early Ellington*. Decca Jazz 1966.

Evans, Bill. *Ultimate Bill Evans*. Verve 1998.

The Fabulous Big Band Collection. RCA Victor 1998.

Fitzgerald, Ella. *Best of the Songbooks*. Verve 1996.

Fitzgerald, Ella. *The Complete Ella in Berlin—Mack the Knife*. Verve 1960.

Fitzgerald, Ella, and Louis Armstrong. *The Best of Ella Fitzgerald and Louis Armstrong on Verve*. Verve 1997.

Getz, Stan. *Ultimate Stan Getz*. Verve 1998.

Gillespie, Dizzy. *Greatest Hits*. Columbia/Legacy 1997.

Hancock, Herbie. *Gershwin's World*. Verve 1998.

Holiday, Billie. *Greatest Hits*. Decca Jazz 1995.

Jazz Greatest Hits of the '20s. RCA Victor 1997.

Krall, Diana. *All For You: A Tribute to the Nat King Cole Trio.* Impulse 1996.

Marsalis, Wynton. *Standard Time.* Columbia 1987.

Mingus, Charles. *Mingus Ah Um.*Columbia/Legacy 1999.

Monk, Thelonious. *Best of the Blue Note Years.* Blue Note 1995.

Morton, Jelly Roll. *Greatest Hits.* RCA Victor 1996.

Parker, Charlie. *Bird's Best Bop on Verve.* Verve 1995.

Prison Songs: Historical Recordings from Parchman Farm 1947–48. The Alan Lomax Collection. Rounder Records 1997.

Ra, Sun. *Futuristic Sound of Sun Ra.* Savoy Jazz 1961.

Rollins, Sonny. *Greatest Hits.* RCA Victor, 1998.

Shepp, Archie. *Live in San Francisco. Impulse 1998.*

Silver, Horace. *Best of.* Blue Note 1988.

Simone, Nina. *The Essential Nina Simone, Vol. I.* RCA 1993.

Smith, Bessie. *The Collection.* Columbia/Legacy 1989.

Swing! Greatest Hits. RCA Victor 1996.

Tatum, Art. *Solos—1940.* MCA 1990.

Vaughan, Sarah. *The Essential Sarah Vaughan: The Great Songs.* Verve 1992.

Wilson, Cassandra. *Blue Light 'Til Dawn.* Blue Note 1993.

Yoruban Drums from Benin, West Africa. Smithsonian Folkways 1991.

For Further reading

Elmer, Howard. *Blues: Its Birth and Growth*. New York: The Rosen Publishing Group, 1999.

Hughes, Langston. *The First Book of Jazz*. Hopewell, NJ: The Ecco Press, 1998.

Oliver, Paul, Max Harrison, and William Bolcom. *The New Grove Gospel, Blues, and Jazz*. New York: W.W. Norton, 1997.

Palmer, Robert. *Deep Blues*. New York: Penguin, 1981.

Savage, Steve. *The Billboard Book of Rhythm*. New York: Billboard, 1989.

Southern, Eileen. *The Music of Black Americans: A History*. 3rd ed. New York: W.W. Norton, 1997.

index

a

Armstrong, Louis, 33–35, 45

b

balaphone, 14–15
ballads, 23, 37, 56
beats, 6, 13–14, 18, 26, 42
bebop, 6, 7, 42, 44, 45, 48, 49, 50, 53
big band, 7, 37–39, 42, 52
blues, 24–25, 34, 37, 38, 43, 47, 48, 49, 51
breaks, 25

c

call-and-response, 13, 18, 21, 36, 38, 50, 56
clarinetists, 30, 36
Coleman, Ornette, 43, 51–52, 53
Coltrane, John, 43, 50–51
Congo Square, 27–29
cool jazz, 47–49
Cotton Club, The, 36–37
Count Basie, 38
Creoles of color, 27, 30

d

dance, 11, 23, 28, 29, 37, 38, 39, 52, 54
Davis, Miles, 48, 50
Dizzy Gillespie, 6, 45
drum, 13–14, 18, 19, 28, 44, 52

e

Ellington, Duke, 35–37, 38, 45, 50

f

field holler, 13, 18, 48
Fitzgerald, Ella, 45, 46
free jazz, 7, 49, 53
frets, 20
fusion, 7, 48

g

griots, 11, 24

h

Harlem Renaissance, 32
Holiday, Billie, 34, 46

i

improvisation, 7, 37, 44, 50, 52, 53

j

Jelly Roll Morton, 26

k

kalimba, 15, 28

l

languages, 10, 12, 14

m

Marsalis, Wynton, 55–56